Decorative
TILE ART

CREATE BEAUTIFUL TILES FOR DISPLAY OR USE

LYDIA D'MOCH

becker&mayer! books

Contents

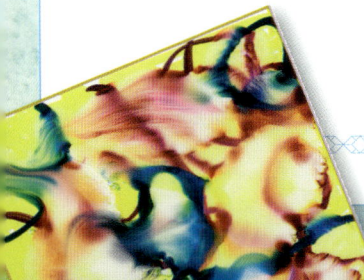

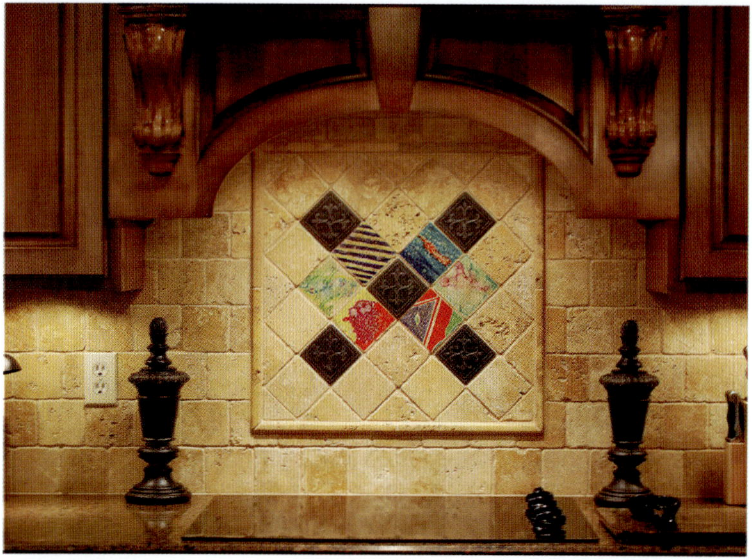

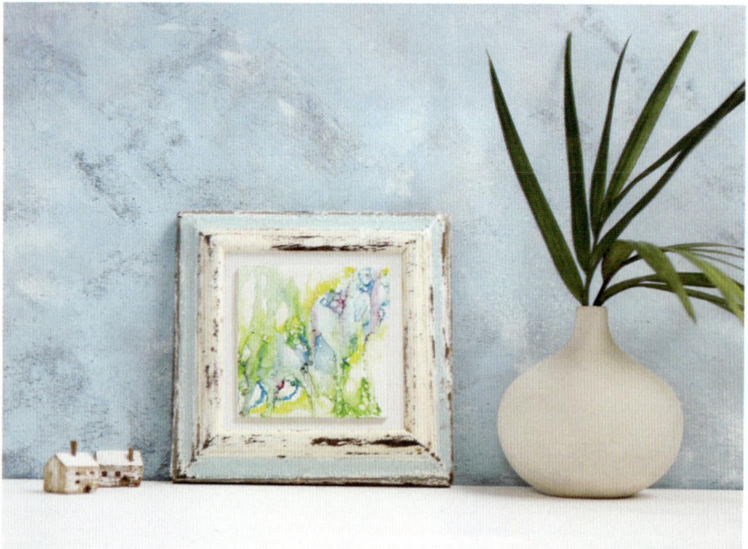

Introduction

Ceramic tiles have been used as a form of decorative art for centuries. Virtually every civilization and culture has created distinctive tile patterns and motifs to embellish homes, public buildings, and gardens.

This kit provides the materials to make four of your own beautifully-decorated tiles. The plain white tiles are the perfect canvas for creativity. Combining permanent markers and everyday isopropyl alcohol on the surface produces fluid, organic, and abstract patterns that make each tile unique.

No art experience is necessary to complete these projects. Simply color the surface of the tile with the markers, then apply alcohol. The ink in the markers will liquefy and blend, blurring together in a vibrant, one-of-a-kind design. You can manipulate the wet ink using the step-by-step instructions included here or try techniques of your own. There is no right or wrong method, and you really cannot make a mistake.

Also included in this kit is a bottle of clear coating to seal your finished tiles, as well a sheet of felt feet that will protect surfaces and allow you to turn your tiles into coasters. What else can you do with your finished tiles? Hang them with an adhesive hook on the back or display them on a shelf. Use them to line the bottom of a tray, or the top of a flea market table. Or frame them!

If you enjoy other crafts such as mosaics, you can also create an endless supply of unique tile fragments for your projects. The tiles you create can be used in countless ways to add a stylish touch throughout your home.

About the Kit

The kit contains the materials to make four decorative tile projects. This 48-page book provides the basic techniques, as well as instructions for additional tile projects that will require a few extra materials.

Included in this Kit:

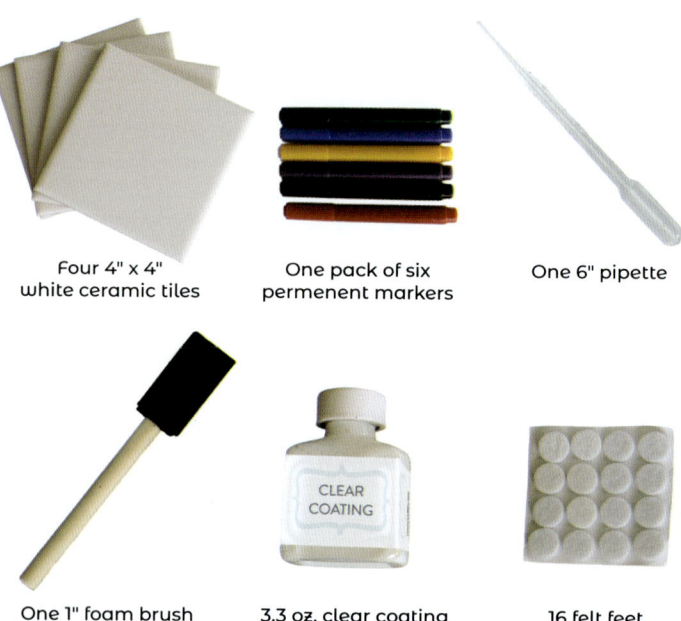

Four 4" x 4"
white ceramic tiles

One pack of six
permement markers

One 6" pipette

One 1" foam brush

3.3 oz. clear coating

16 felt feet

You will also need a bottle of 91% isopropyl alcohol, which can be found at any drugstore. Do not use the lesser grade of 70% isopropyl alcohol (commonly known as rubbing alcohol), because it will not produce a successful result when interacting with the markers.

In addition to the pipette, a spray bottle is used to apply alcohol in most of the projects. Choose a bottle with an adjustable nozzle for spraying either a fine or heavier stream, to create different effects.

Isopropyl alcohol evaporates quickly if left uncapped, so store it with the top on tightly when not in use and keep it away from direct heat. It also has a strong odor, so always use the alcohol in a well-ventilated room, or in an outdoor work area. Also, try to keep the alcohol off of your skin; although a small amount isn't harmful, it can cause irritation and dryness.

Finally, be sure to protect your work surface and have a few paper towels handy for any necessary cleanup. The ink will be runny after the alcohol is applied.

Extra Materials Recommended to Complete Projects in this Book

- Six additional 4" x 4" white ceramic tiles (either gloss or matte finish)

- One bottle of 91% isopropyl alcohol

- One spray bottle with an adjustable nozzle

- One roll of blue painter's tape—2" wide or narrower

- One plastic drinking straw

- Assorted permanent markers in various colors—there are many colors and tip widths available

- A large sheet of paper, cardboard, or a length of foil (to protect surfaces from alcohol sprays and drips, as well as the liquid ink)

Updated Instructions For Best Results

- The liquid clear-coat in this kit is intended to be used to seal tiles that you have drawn designs on but not applied the alcohol technique to.

- If you want to create the tie-dyed effect on your tiles, we do not recommend using the liquid clear coat provided in this kit as it will not give you the optimum result. Instead, to seal your tie-dyed coasters to make them waterproof/colorfast, we strongly recommend applying a coat of spray-on acrylic sealer. The spray-on acrylic can be found at local craft, hobby or hardware stores.

Six 4" x 4"
white ceramic tiles

91% isopropyl alcohol

Spray bottle with an
adjustable nozzle

Blue painter's tape

One plastic drinking
straw

Assorted permanent
markers

About the Technique

The basic technique is the same for all of the projects. First, color the tile surface with the permanent markers, using whatever colors and patterns you like. These projects may specify a color combination or design style for you to try—for example, a solid field of several colors that covers the entire tile, or geometric shapes such as circles or squares. Whatever you choose to draw, no two projects will turn out looking the same.

Next, apply the alcohol using the various methods described here, and watch as the ink liquefies and blends. The ink will be wet as you work, so take care not to touch it to avoid smearing. Also, apply the alcohol sparingly, at first, and wait a few minutes to see how it reacts. The ink will change dramatically in a matter of minutes.

NOTE:
Be sure to work on a completely level surface so that the tile lies flat and the alcohol doesn't pool to one side.

There are many ways to apply the alcohol:

- A pipette or eyedropper releases drops that form liquid pools of ink on the surface.

- A spray bottle is the most versatile tool because you can adjust the nozzle for different effects. Pumping a full spray at close range will dissolve the ink into tendrils and large pools of color. Holding the bottle above the tile, about a foot away, will create a fine mist that dispenses the fewest drops to create small bubbles and stippling on the surface.

- Lifting the tile with your thumb and forefinger and gently rotating it from side-to-side allows the color to run in rivulets that will dry into interesting patterns.

- Blowing through a straw distributes the color in long directional strokes.

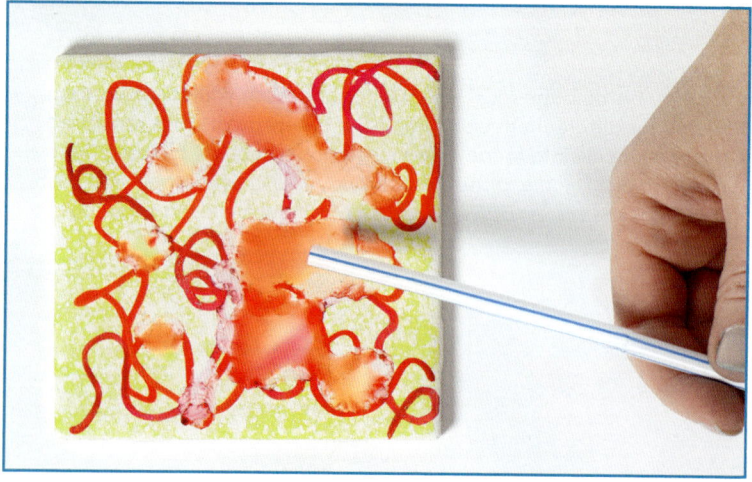

One of the most creative techniques involves building layers of color. Apply alcohol, let the tile dry, and go back and draw with markers again, applying another round of alcohol effects. This is a great way to add richness and depth of color to the tile. If you decide to try this, let the tile dry for at least a half an hour after your first application of alcohol, to preserve the first layer of your design.

A single marker color, applied sparingly with empty white space around it, can net surprising results—and it can be diluted with alcohol and lightly wiped away to create a soft tint.

If you aren't happy with your project and want to try something new, you can simply add drops or spray the tile with the alcohol, wipe it clean, and use it again.

When you are finished with your tile projects, apply a layer of clear coating to protect and preserve them. Let the tiles dry for at least one hour before applying the coating, preferably overnight. The tile may look dry but can still smudge if you touch it, so longer is better.

Pour a quarter-size pool of the clear coating onto a paper plate or piece of foil and use a foam brush to apply a light coat to the surface. Take care to use a light hand with the application, as the brush can leave track marks and possibly affect the design and/or react with the ink. You can also use an acrylic spray varnish as a protective coating to achieve the same result.

Be sure to clean the foam brush when you finish to prevent it from becoming sticky and unusable.

When Alcohol Drops Meet a Tile

Adding drops of alcohol to the tile creates fluid patches of color that continue to evolve as the ink dries.

What You Will Need:

- One 4" x 4" white tile
- One pipette or eyedropper
- One set of permanent markers
- (Optional) One drinking straw
- 91% isopropyl alcohol
- One foam brush
- Clear coating

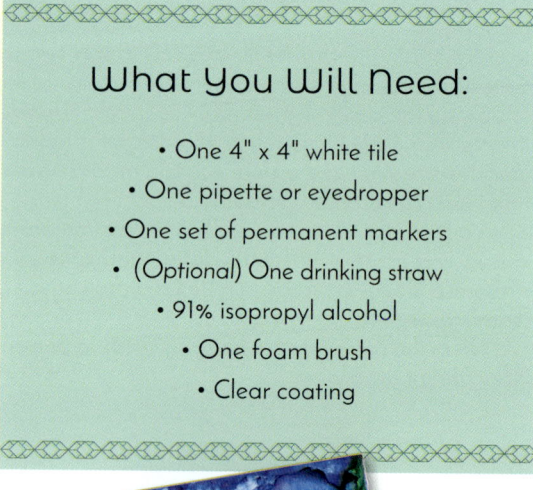

1. Use a blue marker to color the upper left side of the tile on the diagonal. Shown here is a partial triangle with a square cut-out in the center.

2. With the green marker, fill in the square area and the middle of the tile on the diagonal, leaving the lower right corner blank.

3. Color the lower right corner yellow.

4. With the pipette or an eye-dropper, add six to eight drops of alcohol to the surface. The color will begin to break up and spread and will continue to change shape and creep across the surface as it dries.

5. At this point, you can let the tile dry, or add more drops, a few at a time, until you achieve the desired result.

6. When finished, let the tile dry for at least one hour and apply a layer of clear coating to protect and preserve it (see instructions on page 13).

Or, you can try these extra steps:

- While the pools of color from the drops are still wet, gently tilt the tile so the fluid color streams in one direction. Let dry.

- Again, while the pools of color are still wet, blow gently, with or without a straw, directly on the fluid tendrils of paint to redirect their flow across the surface. If you like the effect, let the tile dry.

When Alcohol Spray Meets a Tile

Spraying a fine mist of alcohol onto the surface produces a stippled color blend.

What You Will Need:

- One 4" x 4" white tile
- One extended set of permanent markers
- A spray bottle with an adjustable nozzle
- 91% isopropyl alcohol
- One foam brush
- Clear coating

1. Use three warm shades of markers to cover the tile surface. Shown here is an application of pink in the center, red along the right side from top-to-bottom, and yellow along the outer-left edges.

2. Hold the spray bottle above the tile, about a foot away, and pump the nozzle once to spritz a fine mist on the surface. Notice how the ink separates into a series of droplets.

3. You can stop here if you like. Let dry.

4. When finished, let the tile dry for at least one hour and apply a layer of clear coating to protect and preserve it (see instructions on page 13).

Or, you can try this extra step:

- To create a looser effect with a variety of droplet sizes, add one additional spray of alcohol to the middle of the tile. Let dry.

A Striped Tile

Spraying a fine mist of alcohol and wiping the tile lightly creates a blurred, geometric effect.

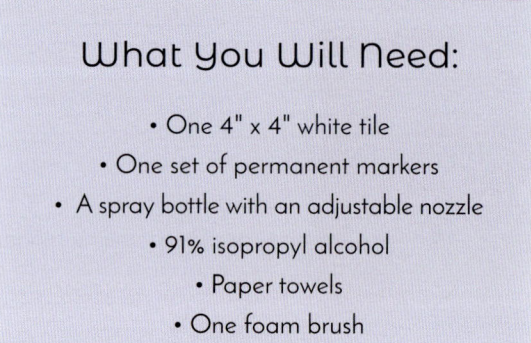

What You Will Need:

- One 4" x 4" white tile
- One set of permanent markers
- A spray bottle with an adjustable nozzle
- 91% isopropyl alcohol
- Paper towels
- One foam brush
- Clear coating

1. Using the purple and yellow markers, draw diagonal lines across the tile, alternating the colors as you go.

2. Hold the spray bottle above the tile, about a foot away, to spritz a fine mist on the surface—one or two pumps will do.

3. Wipe the surface of the tile lightly with a paper towel. Do not rub too hard or you will remove all the pigment.

4. Let dry. You can stop at this point.

5. When finished, let the tile dry for at least one hour and apply a layer of clear coating to protect and preserve it (see instructions on page 13).

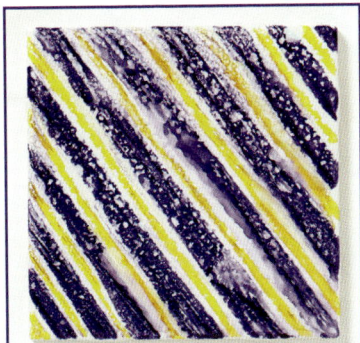

Or, you can try this extra step:

- Apply an additional spray of fine mist to create more of a stippled effect, and to blur the stripes further.

A Field of Diagonal Circles

A field of brightly-colored circles across the diagonal transforms into a cascade of color when alcohol is applied.

What You Will Need:

- One 4" x 4" white tile
- One pipette or eyedropper
- One extended set of permanent markers
- (Optional) One drinking straw
- A spray bottle with an adjustable nozzle
- 91% isopropyl alcohol
- One foam brush
- Clear coating

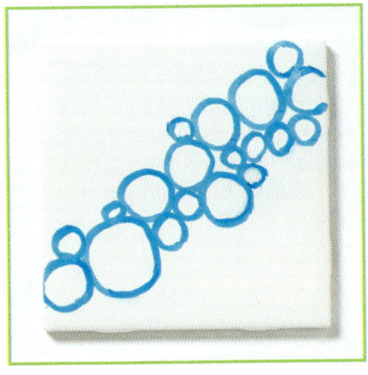

1. Draw a series of 10-12 circles of different sizes diagonally across the tile from lower left to upper right. Medium blue was used here for the outlines of the circles.

2. Add a colored dot to the center of each circle, by alternating pink, ruby red, and orange.

3. Color in a yellow border about 1/2" wide around the perimeter of the circles.

4. Add a small area of light green in the lower right corner and a green accent outside the blue circles.

5. Using the lowest setting on the spray bottle and holding the bottle at least a foot above the tile, spritz a very light application on the tile—no more than a sprinkling of droplets here and there. The circles will begin to break up just slightly. Let dry.

6. Adjust the spray nozzle to dispense a wider field of droplets when sprayed. The shapes should continue to dissolve.

7. Use the pipette to add a few droplets to the center of three or four of the dissolving circles. This should cause the color to run in streaks towards the bottom of the tile.

8. As the streaks form, rotate the tile, so the pattern is upside down, and blow slightly through your lips, or with a straw, to disperse the color further towards the bottom.

9. When finished, let the tile dry for at least one hour and apply a layer of clear coating to protect and preserve it (see instructions on page 13).

PROJECT
5

Using a Stencil Mask

Cutting shapes from painter's tape creates masks that
preserve white areas of the tile surface as ink and alcohol
are applied.

What You Will Need:

- One 4" x 4" white tile

- A cutting mat or piece of
cardboard for cutting tape

- One extended set of permanent markers

- (Optional) One drinking straw

- A spray bottle with an adjustable nozzle

- 91% isopropyl alcohol

- One roll of blue painter's tape
2" width or narrower

- A craft knife

- Two or three cotton swabs, as needed

- One foam brush

- Clear coating

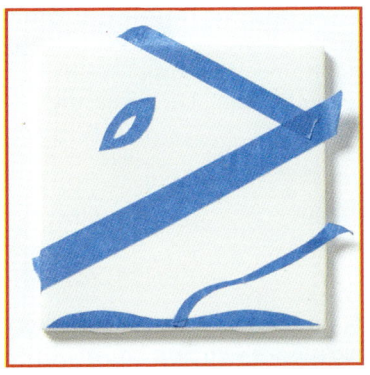

1. Trim a length of blue painter's tape about six inches long and stick it onto a cutting mat or piece of cardboard. With a craft knife, carefully cut a variety of strips and shapes from the tape. Four shapes have been used here—a wide strip, a narrow strip, one with a scalloped edge, and a free-form teardrop shape.

2. Place the tape strips anywhere you like on the surface of the tile. You can use the photo as a guide or create your own design. The taped areas create a mask that preserve the white tile underneath, as you color the surface. For long strips that cover the tile from edge-to-edge, wrap the ends around the sides of the tile to secure them tightly. Burnish the tape with your thumbnail or the edge of a coin to create a tight seal so the alcohol does not penetrate beneath it.

3. Once you've finished positioning the tape, use the markers of your choice to color the tile around the tape. Purple, red, and a touch of light green have been used here.

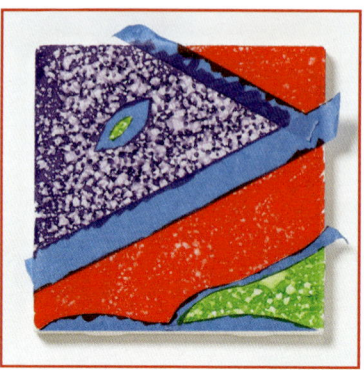

4. Use the fine mist nozzle setting on the spray bottle, and lightly spritz droplets onto the tile surface. Avoid applying too heavy a spray or the ink will dissolve and become runny and may possibly seep under the tape. Let the tile dry.

5. Carefully lift the tape from the tile surface with your fingernail or the tip of a craft blade. You can remove all of the tape or keep some intact if you want to add further effects on another layer.

6. If any unwanted color has seeped into the masked white areas, dip a cotton swab into the alcohol and gently wipe it away.

7. If you like, you can embellish the white areas with drawn details. Here, a line of color was drawn to bisect the white space.

8. If you want to make any changes to the white areas—such as narrowing a line, filling in an edge, or changing the contour—you can do so by filling in your correction with marker ink. Then, to match the alcohol effect on the rest of the tile, hold a piece of paper so it shields the rest of the tile and apply a bit of light spray to the newly-inked area.

9. When finished, let the tile dry for at least one hour and apply a layer of clear coating to protect and preserve it (see instructions on page 13).

A Subtle Blend of Layered Colors

Use several marker colors mixed together to form a solid base color, then wipe off to a light tint. When alcohol is applied, vestiges of the different, blended colors will appear.

What You Will Need:

- One 4" x 4" white tile
- One pipette or eyedropper
- One extended set of permanent markers
- One drinking straw
- A spray bottle with an adjustable nozzle
- 91% isopropyl alcohol
- Paper towels
- One foam brush
- Clear coating

1. Color the tile completely with medium blue, light green, and dark green markers, blending them however you wish as shapes or as an overlapping field of solid color. Use at least three colors.

2. Spray a fine mist of alcohol onto the tile, then use a paper towel to gently rub off most of the color in the middle, which produces a light greenish tint. Leave some color buildup around the edges—you should be able to detect subtle shades of all three colors that were used.

3. Add a squiggle of pink brush-strokes along the center of the tile, radiating downward towards one corner.

4. Add five or six drops of alcohol to the pink line with the pipette or eyedropper. The pink line will swell, pool up, and continue to creep along the surface as it dries.

5. As the pink line transforms, direct the liquid upward from the bottom by blowing with a straw. This mutes the color and creates a wash that will dry without hard edges.

6. When finished, let the tile dry for at least one hour and apply a layer of clear coating to protect and preserve it (see instructions on page 13).

A Geometric Pattern

Rows of alternating shapes and colors are animated by the effect of alcohol spray.

What You Will Need:

- One 4" x 4" white tile
- One extended set of permanent markers
- A spray bottle with an adjustable nozzle
- 91% isopropyl alcohol
- One foam brush
- Clear coating

1. Using light blue and magenta markers, draw a row of five rectangles across the top of the tile in alternating colors. Start the row with a blue box, then alternate across the row.

2. Add five more rows below it to fill the tile with rectangles. Start the second row with a magenta box and alternate across the tile. When finished, you should have five rows with five rectangles in each.

3. Holding the spray bottle about a foot above the tile, dispense a light spritz of alcohol.

4. The boxes should have a stippled effect, but the lines should not run. Let the tile dry.

5. Using lime green and orange markers, apply a dot in the center of each rectangle—lime green dots in the blue boxes, orange dots in the magenta boxes.

6. Add one light spritz of alcohol as you did in Step 3. The lines will thicken and loosen a little with the spray but should not run.

7. When finished, let the tile dry for at least one hour and apply a layer of clear coating to protect and preserve it (see instructions on page 13).

A Southwestern Sunset

Inspired by the colors of a southwestern sunset, this sky twinkles from the effect of alcohol droplets.

What You Will Need:

- One 4" x 4" white tile
- One extended set of permanent markers
- A spray bottle with an adjustable nozzle
- 91% isopropyl alcohol
- One foam brush
- Clear coating

1. Use an orange marker to draw a series of horizontal lines across the midpoint of the tile.

2. Below the orange ink, color in the bottom of the tile using a light blue or aqua marker.

3. Use light blue or aqua above the orange to fill an area about 1-1/2" deep.

4. Fill in the top of the tile with dark blue, blending where the two colors meet. Add a few lines of dark blue at the bottom of the tile.

5. Gently spray the tile with the bottle of alcohol, applying droplets sparingly, until you get the desired effect.

6. When finished, let the tile dry for at least one hour and apply a layer of clear coating to protect and preserve it (see instructions on page 13).

Shape Dissolve

A series of distinct shapes dissolve into fluid fields of color when alcohol is manipulated with a straw.

What You Will Need:

- One 4" x 4" white tile
- One pipette or eyedropper
- One set of permanent markers
- One drinking straw
- A spray bottle with an adjustable nozzle
- 91% isopropyl alcohol
- One foam brush
- Clear coating

1. Draw an undulating diagonal shape in dark blue in the lower right corner of the tile that extends from edge-to-edge, using the photograph as a guide.

2. Add a green undulating shape above the blue shape.

3. In the upper-left corner of the tile, color in a yellow shape. Leave the rest of the tile white.

4. Spray with two pumps of the bottle of alcohol. The colors will erupt in crystallized shapes.

5. With the pipette or eyedropper, add three drops of alcohol in the green and blue area.

6. As the color begins to spread, blow gently with the drinking straw to direct the color into the yellow area. Let dry.

7. Add a few more drops of alcohol in the lower right corner to diffuse the blue and green. As the colors become fluid, use the straw to blow the ink upwards and to the left.

8. The ink will continue to spread over the next few minutes, creating a blue-green flow into the yellow. You can let the colors sit and dry as is, or gently tilt the tile for more color distribution.

9. When finished, let the tile dry for at least one hour and apply a layer of clear coating to protect and preserve it (see instructions on page 13).

Squiggly Line Work

Layers of color, built up in several steps, become a unified whole with a single final spritz of alcohol that adds texture and tonality.

What You Will Need:

- One 4" x 4" white tile
- One pipette or eyedropper
- One set of extended permanent markers
- One drinking straw
- A spray bottle with an adjustable nozzle
- 91% isopropyl alcohol
- One foam brush
- Clear coating

1. Cover the tile surface with yellow marker.

2. Spray a fine mist of alcohol with the spray bottle. Let the tile dry.

3. Draw a series of continuous squiggly lines with red and blue markers, but leave the yellow background visible through the curving lines.

4. Next, using the pipette or eyedropper, place 5–7 drops of alcohol on the title surface. The ink will begin to liquefy.

5. While the ink is still wet and fluid, blow gently with a straw to redirect the flow of the drops. You'll notice that larger pools of color begin to appear.

6. Gently lift the edge of the tile and hold the tile between your thumb and forefinger, rotating very slightly from edge-to-edge to distribute the fluid color. Let dry.

7. Hold the spray bottle about a foot away, and add a light spritz of alcohol from the spray bottle. The fine droplets expand over the surface and the unified effect ties the various colors together.

8. When finished, let the tile dry for at least one hour and apply a layer of clear coating to protect and preserve it (see instructions on page 13).

About the Author

Lydia D'moch has had a successful career as a designer and art director for several publishing houses, specializing in book covers and interiors for the adult and children's trade markets, and collaborating with many of the industry's most well-known authors and illustrators. Her work has earned numerous national design awards and recognition from the AIGA, Bookbuilders West, New York Book Show, PubWest, and the American Library Association. In her spare time, Lydia enjoys crafting and creating in multiple mediums. Lydia lives and works in San Diego, California.

Brimming with creative inspiration, how-to projects, and useful information to enrich your everyday life, Quarto Knows is a favorite destination for those pursuing their interests and passions. Visit our site and dig deeper with our books into your area of interest: Quarto Creates, Quarto Cooks, Quarto Homes, Quarto Lives, Quarto Drives, Quarto Explores, Quarto Gifts, or Quarto Kids.

Published in 2018 by becker&mayer! books, an imprint of The Quarto Group, 11120 NE 33rd Place, Suite 201, Bellevue, WA 98004 USA.
www.QuartoKnows.com

This book is part of the *Decorative Tile Art* kit and is not to be sold separately.

becker&mayer! books titles are also available at discount for retail, wholesale, promotional, and bulk purchase. For details, contact the Special Sales Manager by email at specialsales@quarto.com or by mail at The Quarto Group, Attn: Special Sales Manager, 401 Second Avenue North, Suite 310, Minneapolis, MN 55401 USA.

18 19 20 21 22   5 4 3 2 1

ISBN: 978-0-7603-6211-2

Library of Congress Cataloging-in-Publication Data available upon request.

Author: Lydia D'moch
Design: Susan Elliot and David Brender
Editorial: Lori Asbury
Production: Carolyn McManus
Tile Artists: Hiba Mikdashi and Greg Cook
Photography: Chris Burrows

Printed, manufactured, and assembled in Shenzhen, China, 08/18.

Distributed by:
Quarto UK, The Old Brewery
6 Blundell Street, London N7 9BH, UK
Allen & Unwin
30 Centre Rd, Scoresby VIC 3179, AUS

Image credits: Sunspire/Shutterstock.com, Africa Studio/Shutterstock.com, Godsend/Shutterstock.com, Nik Merkulov/Shutterstock.com, maxim ibragimov/Shutterstock.com, nednapa/Shutterstock.com, Lunatictm/Shutterstock.com, LUQMAN ABU HASSAN/Shutterstock.com, pirtuss/Shutterstock.com, BW Folsom/Shutterstock.com, Winai Tepsuttinun/Shutterstock.com, Gosteva/Shutterstock.com, Melanie DeFazio/Shutterstock.com, sc0rpi0nce/Shutterstock.com, Daria Minaeva/Shutterstock.com, smallsmiles/Shutterstock.com, Todd Taulman Photography/Shutterstock.com, Elizabeth A.Cummings/Shutterstock.com, rachanee angsupasirikul/Shutterstock.com, Yellow Cat/Shutterstock.com, Lunatictm/Shutterstock.com

305122